essential careers™

CAREERS IN
CHILD CARE

JERI FREEDMAN

ROSEN
PUBLISHING

NEW YORK

Published in 2015 by The Rosen Publishing Group, Inc.
29 East 21st Street, New York, NY 10010

First Edition

Library of Congress Cataloging-in-Publication Data

Freedman, Jeri.
Careers in child care/Jeri Freedman.
     pages cm.—(Essential careers)
Includes bibliographical references and index.
ISBN 978-1-4777-7884-5 (library bound)
1. Child care—Vocational guidance—United States—Juvenile literature. 2. Child care—Vocational guidance—Canada—Juvenile literature. I. Title.
HQ778.63.F74 2015
362.70230973—dc23

                                                      2014006851

Manufactured in the United States of America

contents

INTRO

A career in child care offers the chance to help children develop mental and physical skills while providing secure employment.

DUCTION

Since 2008, the economy of the United States has been growing very slowly, and finding a good job has been challenging. Ideally, a job should provide both financial security and personal fulfillment. The child care field can offer secure jobs as well as the opportunity to do meaningful work. There are few activities more important than guiding the development of children. Jobs in child care allow people to make a difference in the lives of young people and help them develop in a positive way. Often, working with children can also be fun, and children see the world in unique ways and are open to new experiences.

The child care field has a strong and steady demand for employees. Because people will continue to have children, it is a field that offers job security. Therefore, even in a stagnant economy, there are excellent prospects for finding a job in this area. Jobs in child care exist for those interested in working with children of all ages, from day care for babies and toddlers to after-school and special programs for young teens. This variety makes it possible to work with children of an age one feels comfortable with. Child care jobs are available in a variety of settings. Among the types of child care facilities are stand-alone child care centers, day care centers in business and government organizations, child care services in institutions such as hospitals, and special child care programs. It is also feasible to run a day care center from one's own home or someone else's.

Jobs exist in child care for those with all levels of education. There are jobs that require only a high school degree and completion of a short training program, positions for those with two- and four-year college degrees, and senior management jobs for those with advanced degrees. This range provides a degree of flexibility, allowing one to start at the entry level, then pursue further training to advance to higher levels of responsibility. In addition, part-time or flexible schedules may be available, depending on the type of facility in which one works. This material will explore the types of facilities in which child care takes place and the various jobs available, including their duties and the training required. Tips on finding and applying for a job in the child care field will also be provided.

chapter 1

CARING FOR CHILDREN

Professional child care has existed as far back as the Middle Ages, when wealthy families hired nurses to care for their children. From the first day nurseries of the nineteenth century to modern day care facilities, child care has evolved. Today, child care takes place in a variety of settings, with children of various ages, and for different purposes.

A HISTORY OF CHILD CARE

Professional child care has a long history. From the Middle Ages through the colonial period, wealthy families hired nurses to care for their children. At this time, the term "nurse" referred to women who watched, fed, cleaned, dressed, and cared for children or the infirm, rather than to those with medical training. By the nineteenth century, these nurses had advanced to become professional nannies who lived in the client's home and provided similar services. Some women with a higher level of skills and education became governesses. In addition to looking after children, these women taught subjects such as reading, writing, history, and arithmetic to their charges.

Formal day care facilities were pioneered in France around the 1840s, with the Société des Crèches ("nurseries") being recognized by the French government in 1869. By the 1850s, day

In the nineteenth century, nannies were employed in middle- and upper-class homes to look after the children. This scene shows a nanny in the nursery tending to the children.

care started to appear in the United States. The first day care center in the United States was the New York Day Nursery, which was formed in 1854. The earliest day nurseries were used primarily by people who were poor and immigrants because the women of these populations had to work. Middle- and upper-class women of the era tended to stay home, but still often employed nannies or governesses to mind their children. By the 1930s, there were eight hundred day nurseries in the United States, but the Great Depression brought about a reduction in charitable contributions and a rise in unemployment, causing two hundred of them to close between 1931 and 1940.

World War II (1939–1945) brought back a demand for day care. As the men went off to war, manufacturing companies turned to women to take over the production of goods needed to support the war effort. As women entered the workforce in large numbers, the demand for day care rose. In 1943, the U.S. Congress allocated $6 million for day care centers for the children of female defense workers. (This amount would be the equivalent of more than $78 million today.) According to "A History of Child Care in the U.S." by Professor Sonya Michel, by 1944, there were 3,000 federally funded community day care centers serving 130,000 children. In some cases companies started to provide their own day care centers. For example, the Kaiser Company set up child service centers at its shipyards in Portland, Oregon. It provided child care, supervised by a well-trained staff, twenty-four hours a day, since the factory ran night as well as day shifts. After World War II, despite pressure to return to the home, many women continued to work, and as the decades passed, more and more entered the workforce. By the late twentieth century, families with two working parents had become the norm. Despite efforts by leaders such as President John F. Kennedy in the 1960s, obtaining government funding for mainstream day care centers turned out to be difficult. Instead, a variety of tax breaks and government subsidies

Children in a war workers' nursery enjoy a midmorning snack. Factories that engaged in the war effort and offered child care enabled women to work in these factories.

for poverty-stricken people were aimed at providing some resources that would allow poor working women to hold jobs. This initiative did little to fill the need for day care for the bulk of the population, and for-profit day care centers began to emerge. These facilities provide day care for a fee, paid by the parents of the children. This model remains the norm in the United States today.

THE OUTLOOK FOR THE CHILD CARE INDUSTRY

According to the U.S. Bureau of Labor Statistics (BLS), the demand for child care workers is expected to grow by 20 percent from 2010 to 2020, which is greater than the average for all occupations. The BLS expects employment of teacher assistants to increase by 15 percent over the same period. The growth in demand will result from increases in the numbers of child care facilities and schools.

The demand for assistant social workers and human service assistants is expected to grow by 28 percent from 2010 to 2020, which is significantly greater than the average for all occupations. Prospects for hiring are good because of an increase in the number of children who require child care and preschool programs. The BLS expects employment of preschool and child care center directors to grow by 25 percent from 2010 to 2020, fueled by continued demand for preschool and child care programs.

JOBS IN CHILD CARE

According to a ChildStats.gov report, *America's Children: Key National Indicators of Well-Being, 2013*, in 2011, 24 percent of children with an employed mother were looked after in a day care center type of facility, such as a day care center, a nursery school or preschool, or Head Start. Another 13 percent were cared for by a home-based child care giver, such as a babysitter, nanny, or au pair. Thus, 37 percent of children of working mothers rely on professional child care.

General Mills provides a child care center in one of the company's locations in Minnesota. More than a third of working mothers rely on child care workers to keep their children happy and healthy. This necessity has created a large number of jobs in child care.

The child care field includes a wide range of jobs in different settings. Some people work in facilities devoted specifically to child care. These include stand-alone day care centers, corporate day care centers, and after-school child care programs. Day care is also provided in other types of facilities, such as government and health care institutions. One can also provide child care in one's own home or be a nanny in someone else's home. Others providing services to children include child life specialists, who work with children in hospital settings, and workers in youth services, such as those who work with troubled, disabled, or runaway children and youths.

The child care field includes jobs for people with all levels of education. It is possible to work in a child care center or social service program, as a child care associate or assistant, with just a high school diploma and possibly a short training program. Other jobs such as day care teacher require a two-year associate's degree, and opportunities exist all the way up to day care center or program director, a position in which people often have at least a bachelor's degree and sometimes advanced degrees. In this field it is possible to start in an entry-level job and then pursue additional training or education to advance to a higher level of responsibility.

chapter 2

CHILD CARE CENTERS

The largest number of child care workers are employed in child care centers. There are different types of child care centers. Some are run for profit; others are nonprofit. Some are stand-alone centers; others are located in companies or other facilities. Some provide care for babies; others cater to young children. Some provide early learning services for underprivileged children. Some provide day care for the children of working parents. Others provide after-school services to school-aged children. The exact positions available and skills required depend on the specific type of facility.

DAY CARE FACILITIES

Child care centers can be for-profit or nonprofit. For-profit child care centers are stand-alone facilities owned and operated by one person or a group of people. They may also be branches operated by a company that owns multiple facilities. The majority of for-profit child care centers are stand-alone facilities owned by one or more individuals who provide the care. For-profit child care centers charge for their services, and the money left over after expenses goes to the people who own the center.

Nonprofit child care centers are operated by churches or synagogues, parent organizations, community groups, charitable organizations, or the government. Nonprofit child care centers may provide services free to their members or the general public, or they may charge a fee to cover their expenses.

In-house child care centers serve the employees of a company. They function similarly to stand-alone child care centers, but the child care providers often receive the same benefits as other employees of the company. An example of an in-house day care center is the Drop Off Center at the Excel Center, a tuition-free school for adults, in Indianapolis, Indiana. The Drop Off Center provides free, temporary, short-term child care for the children (from infants to age twelve) of students at the Excel Center until regular child care can be located. Child care providers who work for major chains or in-house company child care centers often receive benefits such as health insurance in addition to their salary. Benefits vary for those who work for community-based

Children work on art projects at an after-school program for at-risk children. Workers at such after-school programs find them rewarding because they can offer positive activities for children and teach them many essential skills.

nonprofit child care centers or small stand-alone facilities.

One rapidly growing area of child care is extended-day child care centers. These facilities offer services for children after school. With the increasing concern about "latchkey" children—those home alone after school—the demand for such services has been growing. Extended-day facilities include those that simply offer supervised play; facilities providing additional academic instruction or instruction in subjects such as dance, music, computers, or various sports; and teen centers and organizations that provide training and facilities for underprivileged children.

Some people also run day care services in their own homes. Running a day care facility is like running any small business. It requires the owner to know how to keep accounting and tax records, and how to do advertising or marketing to attract clients. Running one's own day care center, either in the home or in a stand-alone building, means that one can keep the profits after paying overhead (expenses necessary to run the business) and the salaries of any workers hired. However, it also means that one is responsible for all the expenses for the business and one's own health insurance. Whether a child care center is located in a home or in a stand-alone facility, it must comply with state and federal regulations.

WHAT'S A CHILD CARE CENTER LIKE?

Child care centers must open early enough for parents to drop off children on their way to work and stay open late

Child care facilities often have outdoor play areas. These areas enable children to get exercise and develop motor skills under the supervision of child care workers.

enough for parents to pick them up after work. Typically, centers are open from 6:00 or 6:30 AM to 6:00 PM, Monday through Friday. Some offer late pickup arrangements for an additional fee. Child care centers will have age-appropriate furniture, toys, and books for children. They often also have

WHY BE A CHILD CARE WORKER?

Why do people become child care professionals and stay in the field? Many feel that the jobs in this field provide a unique opportunity to help children grow and develop.

Peggy Steward, director of a child care facility in Pensacola, Florida, in her book *Childcare Revealed*, has this to say about her job:

"I enjoy going to work each day. One reason is that there are no two days alike; therefore, it is not boring. I always look forward to whatever problems the day will bring for me to solve!

"I could never sit all day behind a desk or in front of a computer. I don't have the strength to drive a truck or to be a construction worker. I would be bored by working a cash register. But, I can sit all day cuddling a child and I do have the strength to push a child on the swing during the play period and the strength of patience."

Molly Thompson, in her *Houston Chronicle* article "Strengths as a Child Care Worker," says:

"It takes a special type of personality to connect with young children on their level and to establish a loving rapport with them. You need to enjoy doing the things children enjoy—playing, being silly, exploring and being creative, for example. The best child care workers find that elusive balance between doing things with and for young children and helping them learn to do for themselves. Smile, play on the floor with them, show sincere affection and be their soft place to fall. If you can do all this day after day, you've got the right outlook to be a child care worker."

The *Princeton Review* article "Career: Child Care Workers" says, "Perhaps the most important characteristic of the child care worker is a delicate balance of maturity and wonder. Child care providers work long hours under trying circumstances with children who are grasping to understand the world. A professional must be mature enough to act responsibly with and around the child but be sufficiently filled with wonder to share in the child's excitement about learning."

an outdoor play area with equipment such as swings, slides, and monkey bars.

RESIDENTIAL AND SPECIAL CHILD CARE FACILITIES

Child care jobs also exist in residential and day facilities for children and youth with special needs. Such facilities include

Working at a child care facility for ill children or children who have disabilities can be fulfilling because one can give children who are dealing with various challenges a chance to enjoy themselves.

residential homes for runaways and troubled youth. There are also both residential and day facilities for children with physical disabilities, developmental disabilities, and conditions such as autism. They may be stand-alone centers or may be located in other institutions, such as a hospital. Residential facilities include accommodations for sleeping and eating, as well as care and learning activities. Like day care centers, these establishments require staff at various levels: aides, assistant social workers, teachers, social workers and counselors, and managers.

chapter 3

PROFESSIONALS IN CHILD CARE FACILITIES

There are a variety of jobs available in child care facilities. Among these jobs are child care associate or aide, assistant teacher, teacher, and director. In addition, positions exist in day and residential facilities for children with special needs, including child life specialists in hospital settings and associates/aides, assistant social workers, social workers, and counselors in facilities providing services for troubled, disabled, or runaway children and youth.

CHILD CARE ASSOCIATES, AIDES, AND ASSISTANTS

Day care facilities employ teachers to provide supervised play and preschool learning activities to children. Day care centers exist for children who range in age from infancy to school age. Teachers are assisted by child care associates, attendants, or aides. Jobs for child care associates can be full- or part-time. Assistants generally require only a high school diploma. Child care associates watch children, ensuring that they stay safe. They serve snacks and help with learning activities. They also update parents about activities and requirements at the day care center. Some day care centers provide early learning activities for underprivileged children to help them do well when they start school. Head Start is a federally funded program that helps children and families engage in early learning activities.

Child care assistants are also employed in after-school programs for school-aged children. Such programs may be provided in schools, such as the Springfield school district before- and after-school child care program, or may be hosted by private organizations such as the Boys and Girls Club. After-school programs are intended to provide safe after-school activities for both children and teens. Some programs may offer additional services such as tutoring, job training, or skills training in areas such as computer science.

SOCIAL SERVICE FACILITIES

Some social service organizations also employ child care workers for children in their programs. For example, the residential substance abuse treatment center of the Salvation Army Family Treatment Services program includes an infant/toddler program that employs caregivers to work with children and mothers in the program. These employees care for the

A child care aide watches a little girl carefully during a bean bag game at a county recreation area that offers supervised activities.

A Day in the Life of a Child Care Worker

What is a typical day like in a child care center? Child care workers must get up very early. They might need to be at the facility by 6:00 or 6:30 AM. Upon arriving, they must prepare the classrooms or play areas; turn on utilities such as heat or air conditioning, as well as office equipment such as computers and copiers; and arrange the supplies for the day. Shortly thereafter, the children arrive. Those who work in play areas or classrooms organize the children for activities such as group play or learning activities. Children in a child care center will need lunch, snacks, and in some cases breakfast or dinner. They will have supervised play time and group activities such as singing and crafts. Generally, weather permitting, there is an outdoor play period, and most facilities have equipment such as slides, swings, and jungle gyms. Most also have one or two nap times. Staff at some child care facilities provide learning enrichment for children. These are activities that are designed to help children develop eye-hand coordination and intellectual skills. Examples of learning activities include art lessons to develop creativity, manipulating toys that help children develop motor skills and learn to recognize patterns, playing games that teach children about colors, and reading early readers or words on flash cards.

If a child gets sick or injured, staff members may have to call the child's parents and/or apply first aid. Staff members may also talk to parents about a child's development or behavior. In some facilities the staff members keep files on each child, tracking his or her activities, behavior, and progress. In some cases, reports are sent monthly or quarterly to parents. Child care workers may also need to prepare informational forms for parents regarding required immunizations or upcoming field trips. At the end of the day, the members of the staff must tidy up the classrooms and facilities so that they are ready for the next day.

children and work with the mothers to develop learning objectives for their children. The caregivers' responsibilities also include providing child care training and encouragement to the mothers and performing screenings to assess the progress of the children.

Sometimes children with challenges such as autism or developmental or physical disabilities remain at home, but they still need assistance with learning daily living skills. Some social service and health care agencies provide personal care assistants who go to people's homes to teach children and teenagers these skills.

DAY CARE TEACHERS

Teachers in day care facilities need to be genuinely fond of children, have a sense of fun, and be able to keep up with a roomful of energetic young children. They must be able to create

Child care teachers help children learn basic skills. Like other teachers, they develop lesson plans, teach, and measure the progress of children to ensure they are developing correctly.

program plans. They must have knowledge of child development to design age-appropriate activities. They also need a
great deal of patience. Spending all day with children can be
rewarding, but it is also demanding. Full-time and part-time
positions exist for day care and preschool teachers. Few day
care centers require teachers to have a bachelor's degree, but
many require a two-year associate's degree. States and provinces
have specific educational requirements. These vary from state
to state (and province to province, in Canada). As an example,
California requires teachers in day care centers to have at least
twelve credits in college-level courses in early childhood education, including a course in each of the following: child
development/psychology; children, family and community;
and curriculum.

THE BUSINESS OF CHILD CARE

Child care centers require people skilled in both child development and management. Directors of child care centers are
usually required to have at least a bachelor's degree in early
childhood education, child development, or a related field.
Larger facilities and those located in schools may prefer the
director to have a master's degree. The director hires and super-
vises teachers and other staff members and is responsible for
the overall management of the center. He or she must have
strong leadership and communication skills, be knowledgeable
about business practices such as making and tracking a budget
and marketing the firm's services, and have a good understanding of child development. The director spends a great deal of
time with staff members designing the curriculum (the activities provided at the center) and with parents of the children.
Some states require directors of day care centers to be certified
by the state. Regulations vary from state to state and province

The director of a day care center explains the operation of a new check-in system. The director is responsible for the overall management of the center, including training of staff members.

to province. As an example, a person may be required to complete a forty-hour course covering aspects of child care, such as proper supervision and proper facility design, including elements such as fences.

Some large day care facilities have a separate business manager, who handles the financial and marketing aspects of the center, while the director oversees the educational side. The business manager, who reports to the director, is responsible for accounting and marketing, sales, and advertising. Day care centers often employ an office manager. The office manager handles payroll, correspondence with parents, ordering supplies, and other non-child-development activities.

SKILLS FOR CHILD CARE PROFESSIONALS

All people working in child care need certain basic skills. They need to understand what activities are appropriate for children of the age they work with, and what skills children of that age are capable of learning and using. The role of child care workers of all sorts is to help the child acquire age-appropriate social, intellectual, and physical skills. The process of a child being able to do more complicated tasks as he or she grows older is called child development. People working with children need to be nurturing and sensitive to the feelings of children. Child care workers must have a genuine interest in and liking for children. They must remain patient even when doing the same activity over and over, facing a misbehaving child, or dealing with difficult parents. They must be organized and able to create structured schedules of activities. At the same time, they must remain flexible and able to deal with unexpected incidents that disrupt the routine.

Some states require all employees who work in child care centers to complete specific requirements within a few months of gaining employment in a child care center. For example, the state of Florida requires all employees of day care centers to take a forty-hour course covering various aspects of proper child care, including health and safety. It is also routine nowadays for states to require child care workers to have a criminal background check, and in some cases to be fingerprinted, to ensure the safety of the children in their care.

PROVIDING CHILD CARE AT HOME

Some people, primarily women, choose to provide child care services in their home. Providing child care in one's home is more than just babysitting. One must be prepared to see to multiple children's needs all day long. The preparation encompasses becoming familiar with child development activities and setting up a schedule of activities, including feeding and nap times. As with any business, running a child care service means billing clients and making sure one is paid. Providing child care services also requires keeping records about each child and supplying this information periodically to clients. Those who choose to deliver

The operator of a home-based day care center prepares children to play outside. Providing day care in her home allows her to spend time with her own children while making an income.

child care in their home must be aware of their state's regulations regarding child care providers and facilities and make sure they comply with safety regulations and health rules. Child care resource and referral agencies provide information to parents on child care resources. They also provide information to individuals on setting up a home child care service. The National Association of Child Care Resource and Referral Agencies (http://www.naccrra.org) can provide information on such agencies. In Canada, the Canadian Child Care Federation (http://www.cccf-fcsge.ca) provides similar information.

CHILD CARE IN SPECIAL NEEDS FACILITIES

A variety of schools, camps, shelters, and day and residential facilities exist for children of all ages with special needs. These facilities may cater to children with physical or developmental disabilities. Others cater to children with disorders such as autism or psychological problems. At day facilities, children attend during the day and go home at night. At a residential facility, children live in the facility. Attendants/personal care assistants in these settings provide children with guidance and assistance with daily living activities, such as dressing and eating. These facilities also employ assistant social workers, social workers and counselors, teachers, and teachers' aides. Teachers' aides help teachers train children in educational subjects and in practical skills, learning how to care for themselves and function in the real world. Personal care assistants are assigned to an individual child and provide support to him or her throughout the day, in the classroom, traveling between rooms, in the cafeteria, in play areas, and on field trips. Personal care assistants document the child's behavior, ensure that he or she is safe at all times, and intervene if the child gets out of control. They see that the child practices the activities assigned by teachers, and supervise social activities. Assistant social workers and social workers support and assist children's families and help arrange services for children and their families. Social workers and counselors help children adjust to their condition and develop the skills they need to live in the community. Assistant teachers and teachers teach the children both academic and practical skills.

Child life specialists work primarily in hospitals. They address the emotional, social, and developmental needs of

A child life specialist engages a hospitalized child in play. Child life specialists help children deal with the stress of hospitalization and medical procedures.

young patients. Children in hospitals often have a great deal of fear and anxiety. One of the main goals of child life specialists is to provide support and activities that help hospitalized children adjust to being in the hospital. They provide developmental play activities for children who are hospitalized for an extended period. However, they do much more. They teach children and their parents about medical procedures and help calm and distract children during such procedures. They offer information and support to parents of hospitalized children. They help children deal with the death of a loved one. They assist in the emergency room, calming children and helping with procedures on children, for example, holding or distracting children during medical tests. They help children prepare for medical procedures and engage them in therapeutic play to deal with their fear. Increasingly, child life specialists are being employed in nonhospital facilities such as camps and schools for children with special needs, and hospices (long-term care facilities for people with incurable illnesses).

chapter 4

BEING A NANNY

Whereas many child care workers are employed in their own home or a child care center or other facility, nannies work alone in someone else's home. Being a nanny means being totally responsible for someone else's child or children. Most nannies are female, but there are some male nannies. Nannies may care for babies or young children. Unlike babysitters, who merely attend to children's basic needs and make sure they are safe, nannies engage children in a variety of activities inside and outside the house. Some nannies undergo special training so that they can help in the development of the children they care for. An au pair is a person who lives in the home of a family abroad and performs the activities of a nanny. Taking a job as an au pair can provide the opportunity to experience the culture of another country, while reducing the cost of travel. However, one must be responsible about one's job caring for the children of the family with which one stays.

WORKING AS A NANNY

Some nannies live in their employers' home. Others come to the house on a daily basis. Nannies work long hours but often have weekends and holidays off. Nannies may work full-time or part-time, and they may be employed on a permanent basis or for a specific period of time—for example, when a parent is

A nanny goes sledding with the child she looks after in the park. Nannies participate in a wider range of activities with their charges than workers at day care facilities do.

hospitalized. Nannies plan and supervise the daily activities of the children they care for. Nannies tend to children's physical needs. Among other activities, they wash and dress children and see that they get appropriate exercise. They prepare meals for children and make sure that they eat. They take children on outings. They engage children in play activities designed to stimulate their mental development and social skills. They are responsible for appropriately disciplining children when they misbehave. They may be responsible for transporting children to lessons and sports activities. In some cases, they may also be responsible for housekeeping activities related to child care, such as tidying up children's rooms and/or doing the children's laundry.

Some nannies specialize in a particular area. For example, some specialize in the care of newborn babies. These nannies are trained in the care of newborns and often provide twenty-four-hour care for families with newborns. A governess is a nanny with educational credentials who provides home schooling or tutoring to the family's children. A governess is concerned chiefly with educating children and does not usually perform basic care or housekeeping tasks.

A DAY IN THE LIFE OF A NANNY

Nannies may be responsible for a single child or multiple children. In a household with multiple children, the nanny must feed and dress any school-aged children and escort them to the school bus stop if necessary. The nanny then spends the morning with younger children. She will supervise their play and may read to them. She will most likely take them outside to play or on an outing to a location such as a park. She will prepare the children's lunch and have them take naps. She will tidy up after the children. When older children return home, she will see that they do their homework and any chores assigned to them. She may prepare dinner for the children or simply accompany them to the family meal. After dinner she may leave to go home, or if she is a live-in nanny, prepare the children for bed.

DO YOU HAVE WHAT IT TAKES?

Certain personal traits and skills are required to succeed as a nanny. Nannies must be nurturing and have the ability to sense the needs of children. However, they must also be able to see that children behave well. They must be able to remain calm in difficult situations and have great patience. They must also be able to work on their own without the support of coworkers that child care workers in day care centers have. In addition, they must be able to adapt to new and changing situations. Nannies also require knowledge of child development and activities that help children develop age-appropriate skills. A nanny must be able to communicate about the child to the

Nannies take their charges for a walk. Although they do not have the company of coworkers, nannies in a neighborhood often get to know and support one another.

parents orally and in writing. A nanny must have a professional appearance and good manners. She must respond to parental requests in a timely manner. A nanny must be able to keep the children in her charge safe and respond to emergencies.

The following is a summary of a series of standards (guidelines for behavior) developed by the International Nanny Association (INA):

- Nannies should respect each child as a unique individual and create an environment that fosters each child's self-esteem and independence. They should use developmentally appropriate behavioral techniques to build trusting relationships with their charges.

- Nannies should provide developmentally appropriate play and learning experiences to enhance the children's physical, emotional, intellectual, and social skills. They should model acceptable language and encourage the development of language skills.

- Nannies should create and maintain a safe and healthy environment for children.

- Nannies should have knowledge of childproofing techniques and know how to meet a child's physical and emotional needs. They must be able to communicate at the child's level of understanding and engage him or her in activities.

This photograph shows a childproof latch. Nannies often must look after children too young to understand the dangers around them. Nannies must know how to keep the children safe.

- Nannies should respect the family's right to privacy and keep confidential any information they learn about the family.
- Nannies should respect the child-rearing philosophy of their clients and acknowledge the ultimate authority of parents in making decisions about the welfare and care of their child/children.
- Nannies should develop a positive relationship with the family, working cooperatively with the family, performing their duties as agreed, communicating openly and effectively, showing sensitivity to family situations, seeking constructive solutions to problems, and maintaining a positive attitude.

In addition to these guidelines, the INA recommends that nannies be familiar with the signs of child abuse and neglect, and the procedures for reporting abuse and neglect. According to the INA, "Nannies are court-mandated reporters and have a professional and ethical obligation to report suspected abuse of any child to the proper authorities."

chapter 5

EDUCATION FOR CHILD CARE CAREERS

E ducation for careers in child care ranges from programs that take several months to one year to two-year associate's degree programs to four-year teaching degrees, and in the case of head teachers or directors of a facility, sometimes advanced degrees. Certification from professional organizations for child care professionals and nannies provides demonstrated proof of competency and can aid applicants in obtaining a job. There is a wide range of educational resources with programs in child care, including technical and vocational schools, online programs, nanny schools, and community colleges and conventional colleges.

HIGH SCHOOL PREPARATION

High school is a time to obtain a broad general education. The more subjects you understand, the better equipped you will be to understand and work with people. Having a knowledge of history, math, and science is beneficial. When working in child development, one is often called on to explain basic facts and principles and to design activities that develop skills in a variety of intellectual areas. A solid high school education will equip you to understand the content of child development programs.

Child care is a field in which one is constantly communicating with children, parents, and coworkers. Therefore, it is

This high school student (far left) *is taking a day care training program that is offered by her school. Students who are interested in pursuing careers in child care learn how to engage children in real-life, hands-on situations. Such training provides students with both skills and experience.*

vital to learn to communicate well both verbally and in writing. Documenting children's progress in written form is a part of most child care jobs. In addition, young children model their speech on their primary caregiver's. To ensure their charges learn to communicate properly and clearly, child care professionals must do so themselves. Learn the rules of English grammar and composition and how to communicate ideas clearly. If your school offers computer training, take advantage of that as well, since computers are used everywhere today for both documentation and interactive training of children.

START PREPARING NOW

Child care is an area in which there are a large number of opportunities to gain experience while a person is in high school. The most obvious way to gain experience is through babysitting. Babysitting can provide the opportunity not only to earn money but also to see if one enjoys working with children and to practice ways of engaging them. There are, however, other ways to gain experience. One can obtain a summer job as a camp counselor. Private and non-profit organizations hire teenagers as camp counselors who conduct indoor and outdoor activities with children. Many city parks and recreation departments hire teenagers as counselors for summer programs they hold for younger children. In this job, one organizes sports and recreational activities.

Volunteering in a summer or after-school reading program for children or obtaining a summer position as a camp counselor is an excellent way to gain experience working with children.

Contact the city or state parks and recreation department in your area for information on part-time jobs.

One can also tutor younger students on subjects in which one has expertise. Most schools have a tutoring program for which they are seeking volunteers. A great way to gain expertise is to work as a volunteer with a program such as Big Brothers Big Sisters, the local Boys and Girls Club, or other children's charities. Working as a volunteer for a charitable organization allows one to help people and contribute to the community while learning skills for dealing with children. Gaining experience while you are in high school will give you a head start when dealing with children on the job. In addition, it will provide you with experience for a résumé or job application and people who can write references for you when you begin to look for your first job.

For the same reason, if your school offers a typing or keyboarding course, take it because it will make your work on the computer more efficient. Because of the multicultural nature of the United States and Canada, the children being cared for are likely to come from various ethnic backgrounds. Therefore, it is very useful to know a second language. In the United States the second most common language is Spanish; in Canada, it is French. Depending on the ethnic makeup of the area in which one works, those with a mastery of other languages may also be in demand.

In many towns and cities, there is both a regular high school and a technical or vocational high school. In others, the single high school offers a technical or vocational program in addition to the traditional high school program designed to prepare students for college. If you think there is a high probability that you will enter the workforce after completing high school, rather than go directly to college, consider pursuing a technical or vocational program in child care if one is offered.

COLLEGE TRAINING

Students who do not enter the child care field directly out of high school, or who wish to pursue further education part-time while working, can take either two-year or four-year college programs. Many community colleges offer a two-year associate of arts (AA) degree in early childhood education. In addition to classes in early childhood education, students take classes in subjects such as English, mathematics, history, and science. In most cases students who get an AA degree can transfer all or most of their credits to another college or university if they decide to pursue a four-year bachelor's degree. It's usually not necessary to have a bachelor's degree to work as a teacher in a child care center. However, getting one can give one an edge when applying for a job and make it easier to move up the ladder to positions such as assistant director and director. The National Association for the Education of Young Children

These students are enrolled in a nanny school, where they are learning child care skills. When they complete their training, they will be eligible for nanny certification.

maintains a list of accredited associate's degree programs in early childhood education on its website (https://www.naeyc.org/ecada/ecada_programs). It is also possible to complete coursework online. If one takes the online approach to obtaining a two-year associate's degree, it is a good idea to check the U.S. Department of Education's online database of accredited schools (http://ope.ed.gov/accreditation/Search.aspx) to ensure that the school is accredited.

There are many training programs for nannies. Such programs generally offer classes in child development, nutrition, family dynamics, play activities, and first aid and cardiopulmonary resuscitation (CPR). Typically they have a practical component that includes supervised interaction with children as well as classroom courses. The International Nanny Association maintains an online directory of placement agencies and training program at http://www.secure.nanny.org/business-directory. Students in such programs receive a certificate upon finishing the program.

Child life specialists must complete a bachelor's degree program in an area such as education, psychology, or child development. The program will include an internship in a hospital as well as coursework. To become a director of a child life program, one must have a master's degree.

Many of those who wish to work as assistant social workers, in programs for disadvantaged children, troubled youth, or children with special needs obtain two-year associate's degrees in social work. They can continue their education to obtain a four-year bachelor's degree to become a social worker. In

A student practices cardiopulmonary resuscitation during a CPR course. Passing a CPR course can prepare a child care worker to deal with an emergency involving a child.

many cases, courses can be taken part-time while these individuals are working.

Because accidents are common when working with children, many employers prefer job candidates with certification in CPR and first aid. Courses are available from the AmericanRed Cross, and its website (http://www.redcross .org/take-a-class/program-highlights/cpr-first-aid) provides a list of classes they offer by location.

CERTIFICATION FOR CHILD CARE PROFESSIONALS

Certification in the field of child care can improve one's chances of obtaining a job and advancing in the field. Certification assures potential employers and the parents of children that a candidate for a job has the proper training and experience. The Council for Professional Recognition offers the Child Development Associate certification. To apply, one must have a high school diploma and 480 hours of child care experience. However, high school students who are juniors or seniors in vocational-technical programs can apply for certification after they complete 120 hours of child development education and have completed 480 hours of child care work. High school students must have questionnaires filled out by the parents of children they've worked with, prepare a portfolio illustrating their work, and provide a letter and transcript from their school. Forms and information on what to include are available from the council's website (http://www.cdacouncil.org/ the-cda-credential). Applicants are tested on their knowledge of six areas of child development:

- How to establish and maintain a safe and healthy learning environment
- How to advance physical and intellectual competence, including developing children's physical, intellectual, communicative, and creative skills
- How to support social and emotional development and provide positive guidance

- How to establish positive relationships with the families of the children in one's care
- How to ensure a well-run, purposeful program responsive to participants' needs through program management
- How to maintain a commitment to the field through professionalism

In addition to performing coursework, applicants are watched during their work by an observer, who evaluates them. Upon completion of certification, the applicants are mailed a certificate. Certification must be renewed every three years and must be in the same setting/age-level endorsement and specialization.

Another organization that provides certification is the National Early Childhood Program Accreditation Commission, which offers the Certified Child Care Professional certification. This certification is designed for teachers who want proof of their knowledge and skills in early childhood development. Those applying for certification must supply evidence of academic training, such as a high school diploma or GED, transcripts from schools where they took courses, and the like. They must have 720 hours of experience in a licensed child care program or school. They are also asked to provide a professional portfolio containing items such as letters of recommendation, parent evaluation forms or other forms of recognition, writing samples, and other professional information. They must complete 180 hours of training, be observed by a field counselor, take the National Credentialing Examination, and undergo a Professional Standards Council Review. The certification must be renewed periodically. More information can be found on the commission's website (http://www.necpa.net/ccp.php).

A student of a nanny and governess school is doing the practical part of her training at a family's home. Formal nanny educational preparation and certification allows a nanny to prove that she is properly trained and qualified.

The International Nanny Association offers the Nanny Basic Skills Exam and the Nanny Credential Exam. The Nanny Basic Skills Exam covers health, safety, nutrition, professionalism, and child development. The INA Nanny Credential Exam is more extensive and demanding. The INA recommends that participants have two thousand hours of experience (one year of full-time work) prior to taking the exam. Applicants must also have a current certification in infant/child CPR and first aid, and photo identification (ID). The exam consists of ninety questions covering child development, family/provider communication, child guidance, multicultural/diversity awareness, learning environment, personal qualities of a nanny, safety, management skills, health, nutrition, and professionalism.

Child life specialists are certified by the Child Life Council through the Certified Child Life Professional exam. This certification is required to work in the field. To be eligible for this examination, applicants must have completed a bachelor's degree, including ten courses in child life/ development areas and 480 hours of practical work.

PROFESSIONAL ORGANIZATIONS

Those who do best in their careers stay current with developments and opportunities in their field. One of the best ways to continue to learn and stay relevant in the field is by joining a professional industry organization, such as the National Association for the Education of Young Children (NAEYC) or the International Nanny Association (INA). These organizations hold conferences and workshops for members. Joining this type of organization also provides the opportunity to discuss issues and problems with other professionals. As your experience grows, you will have the chance to enhance the industry by sharing your knowledge with others.

chapter 6

LANDING A JOB

O nce a person has decided to pursue a position in the child care field, the next step is to find a job. One can use a variety of resources to locate jobs, but first it is necessary to prepare a résumé, which provides potential employers with information on one's experience and education. If the résumé convinces a potential employer that an applicant might be a good fit for a job, the next step is a job interview. This section covers all these aspects of job hunting.

FINDING A JOB

How one goes about finding a job in child care depends on whether one is seeking to work in a child care facility or as a nanny. Some sources of job information apply to both types of careers, but there are some resources that are specific to nannies.

One way to locate child care jobs is to search want ads in either online or print versions of newspapers. Because of the high demand for child care workers and frequent turnover (people leaving jobs), one may find a position in this way. However, the number of people responding to each ad is large, so there is a great deal of competition. Therefore, it is worth pursuing other avenues of job searching as well.

One of the most common ways of finding jobs today is through online job hunting sites. These sites are preferred by many companies today for advertising job openings. Such sites

Today, both professional child care/nanny organizations and general job hunting sites provide online advertisements for child care workers and nannies. There are also print ads in newspapers for some agencies.

include Monster.com and CareerBuilder.com, among others. One can choose specific types of jobs to search for or a general category such as "child care." Using a more general search term allows one to view many types of child care jobs at various types of facilities. This approach may provide one with information on jobs in child care that wouldn't otherwise be apparent. If there are large organizations or chains of child care facilities in an area, one can go to that company's website as well. Most companies have a link called "Jobs" or "Career," which one can click to see job openings.

It is also worth checking out the websites of professional child care and nanny organizations. These sites often have a link to a section of the site that lists jobs and/or offer referral services for facilities interested in hiring.

If one takes a course as part of the preparation for a child care career, the school may offer job placement resources. Technical schools, community colleges, and four-year colleges usually have a job placement office that helps students locate jobs. The school placement office may also provide training in job hunting skills and assistance in preparing résumés.

There is a high turnover in child care jobs, and the increasing demand for services creates a continuous need for additional staff members. As a result, child care centers frequently develop openings for personnel. Many facilities accept applications for positions on-site. It is possible to obtain a list of child care centers in one's area from the local phone book. One can call these companies to see if positions are available. It is often worth sending a résumé to the director or human resources department of facilities, even if they are not advertising for staff. Facilities often keep a file of promising résumés and call applicants when an opening occurs. Thus, even if a job isn't immediately available, one may get a call when a position opens up. Many child care facilities use substitutes when a regular employee is not available due to illness or an emergency. Ask if the facility employs substitutes and, if so, ask to be put on the list. Another approach is to look for a part-time job, possibly while still in school. When a full-time position opens up, many facilities give preference to current part-time employees.

NANNY AGENCIES

Advertisements for nannies can be found in general job search sites and want ads. However, most nannies are hired via a nanny agency. A nanny agency can be a brick-and-mortar company or an online agency. The major difference is that brick-and-mortar agencies typically interview both the nannies and the families interested in hiring one. The agency then tries to make an appropriate match. The online agencies typically list information about the nannies available and/or jobs with families looking to hire a nanny, and leave it up to the parties involved to contact each other and see if they are a good fit. NannyNetwork.com maintains a database of nanny agencies. Standards for nannies vary from agency to agency. Some have a minimum age of eighteen; others take only those twenty years old or older. Typically, agencies

have requirements for a certain level of education and training and experience. They require clean criminal and driving records, and may have health-related requirements such as vaccinations or a negative tuberculosis test. To register with an

Many families prefer to hire a nanny through a nanny agency because these agencies perform background, academic, and reference checks on the nannies, ensuring they are qualified.

agency, one must complete an application and provide references who can be contacted.

BRICK-AND-MORTAR NANNY AGENCIES

When brick-and-mortar agencies have a job that may be appropriate for a candidate, they provide a profile of the job and family. If the candidate is interested, the agency arranges an interview with the family. If the family wishes to hire the candidate, the agency presents an offer from the family. If the candidate agrees to accept the job, the agency assists in drawing up a work agreement. This agreement spells out the services the nanny will provide and the compensation and other terms of employment. The agency will also run a criminal background check on the nanny. About one to four weeks after the job begins, the agency will follow up to make sure things are going well for both the client and the nanny. If there are issues at any time, however, the nanny can contact the agency for assistance. The brick-and-mortar agency's fees for finding a nanny are paid by the family.

ONLINE NANNY AGENCIES

There are a number of online sites for nannies. The site 4nannies.com is oldest of these. Some other sites include eNannySource.com, NannyPro.com, and GoNannies.com. When accessing an online agency, it is a good idea to verify that it is a member of a recognized organization, such as the International Nanny Association or Better Business Bureau. This confirmation reduces the chance that it is a phishing site run by Internet scammers and designed to capture people's personal information. When you register with an online agency or respond to contacts through the site, never give out your Social Security or driver's license number. Your

Social Security number will be needed by an employer for tax purposes, but there is no legitimate reason to ask for this information prior to accepting a job. Online agencies charge the families a fee to access the service. Some also charge nannies a small fee to list their information. Legitimate agencies charge only a minimal listing fee at most. Be wary of any site or ad that claims it will get you a job if you pay them a fee, especially a large one. These are most likely scams.

When scheduling an interview with a prospective family, choose a public place, such as a restaurant or coffee shop. Bring your résumé and contact information about the people who have agreed to give references for your work.

To register with an online agency, applicants fill out a questionnaire with basic information such as name, address, and phone number; information about their background; and often essay-style questions designed to reveal information about their personality. Depending on the site, families may contact nannies who interest them, and/or nannies can contact families with a job that interests them. After making contact, the family will most likely request an interview, along with a résumé and references. Because no one has prescreened the people applicants meet online, it is often best to schedule a first meeting in a public place, such as a coffee shop. If there is mutual interest, one can request references from the family, too, and if possible the names and phone numbers of previous caregivers. If a job offer is made, one should have the family provide in writing the amount of pay, duties, hours, and benefits, such as paid vacation. The family will want to do a criminal and driving check on the candidate as well. At that time, the nanny can provide a Social Security number.

PREPARING A RÉSUMÉ

When applying for a job, applicants need to provide potential employers with a résumé. This document lists one's skills, experience, and training. The résumé's purpose is to convince a potential employer to grant the applicant an interview. Therefore, the résumé should focus on the skills that apply specifically to the jobs being applied for.

Create a résumé in a simple, easy-to-follow format. Start with personal information such as name, address, phone number, and e-mail address. Then list any jobs held, with the most recent first. In child care, list any part-time and summer jobs you have had, including volunteer and unpaid tutoring jobs. In the child care field, volunteer positions involving children demonstrate valuable experience.

TIPS FOR NANNIES

The following recommendations are based on those at NannyNetwork.com (www.nannynetwork.com) for those seeking jobs in child care:

- Listen to your instincts. If you are uneasy for any reason, move on to another opportunity.
- Communicate: Make sure you have been clear about hours, duties, child-rearing philosophies, and compensation before you start work. At work be realistic about what you can accomplish, and prioritize, doing the most important things first.
- Document: Write a work agreement, which should be signed by the nanny and the family. Keep a copy and review it periodically. If families add duties, additional compensation should be agreed upon.
- Be a professional: Provide your employer and the children with the best possible child care. Keep a nanny log or daily journal to provide information to the family. Show up on time and be ready for work. Continue to expand your knowledge of child development and education by reading books, attending seminars, and joining nanny associations.

Next, list your education. Include any certificate or degree courses you have taken, and list any certifications you have obtained. Include vocational courses completed in high school.

If you speak a language other than English, list this as well. With the vast numbers of non-English-speaking children and parents in the child care system, being bilingual can be a major advantage when applying for a job. Likewise, if

Sonya Alvarez
500 East Street
Worcester, MA 01610
(508) 555-1212
SonyaAlvarez@internetprovider.com

OBJECTIVE: Child care associate or assistant teacher position

Day Care Qualifications and Competencies

- Excellent interpersonal communication abilities allow for effective interaction with children and adults
- Interact easily with people of diverse backgrounds, cultures, and professions
- Get along well with children of all ages from newborns to preschool
- Current First Aid and CPR Certification
- Fluent in Spanish
- Possess good computer skills and ability to teach basic skills

EXPERIENCE

Tutor, Catch-Up Training Centers, Worcester, MA 2014

- Tutored children ages 6–10 in reading to bring their comprehension up to an age-appropriate level

Assistant Counselor, Fun-Days Summer Camp, Summer 2013

- Supervised children during outdoor activities
- Provided children with information and instruction as assigned
- Assisted teachers in meeting children's physical, psychological, and nutritional needs

Volunteer, Children with Special Needs After-School Program, Worcester, MA 2012–2013

- Interacted with children in a positive manner
- Supervised children and engaged them in age-appropriate activities
- Arranged equipment and supplies for teachers and students
- Escorted children to activities as instructed

Babysitter, Worcester, MA 2010-2013

- Provided care to multiple children for numerous families
- Changed diapers and tended babies
- Served food to children
- Prepared children for bed
- Supervised children's play and ensured their safety

EDUCATION

Graduate: City High School, Worcester, MA 2013
Certificate in early child care and development, Worcester Community College, 2014

COMPUTER SKILLS

Microsoft Word, Excel, and PowerPoint

References available on request

This example shows one way to format a child care résumé. Although the formats of résumés vary, they should all highlight skills, experience, and educational qualifications specific to the field.

you have completed a CPR and first-aid course, include that information, too.

Be sure to proofread your résumé—or better yet, have someone else read it. People will be trusting you with the health and safety of their children. You do not want to give potential employers the impression that you are careless or sloppy by sending them a résumé with mistakes in it.

INTERVIEWING FOR A CHILD CARE JOB

The interview provides you with the opportunity to convince a prospective employer to hire you. How you present yourself has a significant effect on whether or not you are hired. Make sure your clothing is neat, clean, and professional looking, and that you are well groomed. Even if you are applying for a job where you will wear a smock or a uniform, make sure you are dressed like a professional at the interview. Looking like a professional makes other people see you as one. It is not appropriate to wear loud makeup or jewelry, piercings, or tattoos. The same applies once you have obtained a job. If your job does not require wearing a uniform, always dress neatly and appropriately.

When meeting prospective employers, one should speak respectfully and use correct grammar. Be polite to everyone you meet because prospective employers are evaluating you for your people skills and compatibility as well as your practical skills. If you are asked about experience or skills you don't have, explain how your education or background equips you to learn those skills. Often interviewers ask questions designed to see how a candidate will react under stress or analyze problems. Describe how you would break the problem down to solve it and/or contact an appropriate resource for assistance.

Practice answering difficult questions in advance, such as, "Why do you want to work here?" or "What are your weaknesses?" This preparation will allow you to answer them fluently when you are asked. The following are examples of how to answer tough child care interview questions from Rachel Carpenter's Yahoo! article "Sample Interview Questions for a Child Care or Day Care Worker":

What type of child care situation do you think you cannot handle?
This interview question will help a future boss learn more about your personality. A good answer might be "I feel that I can adapt in all situations. I think some might be more challenging than others, but I am confident that I could handle any situation. However, I would be uncomfortable in situations that go against child care licensing standards, such as teacher/child ratio."

What would you do if a parent was very upset that her child got hit by another child?
The child care director will want to know how you would handle difficult scenarios. One good response for this question is "I would calmly tell the parent that I can understand why they are frustrated. I would say that we are doing everything possible to prevent this from happening again, such as having daily lessons on being nice to our friends."

Be prepared to give examples of situations in which you demonstrated responsibility, carried out tasks unsupervised, and dealt with difficult situations. Even if not asked specifically about this, it's useful to let prospective employers know that you appreciate the need for responsibility and reliability and have demonstrated this in the past. Be sure to thank everyone and show that you appreciate the opportunity.

CONTINUING YOUR DEVELOPMENT

After you obtain a job, you should continue to develop and improve your skills by reading books and journals and by attending workshops and conferences offered by industry organizations. If you are a nanny and work alone, you might want to join one of the online nanny support groups where you can share ideas with others in your field. Staying current with the field can provide you with a rewarding career for many years and increase your chances of advancement.

glossary

accredited Having official approval to do something, particularly because of having reached an acceptable standard.

age-appropriate Suitable in size or complexity for a child of a specific age.

anxiety Nervousness.

au pair A person who lives with a family abroad and provides nanny services.

autism A complex brain disorder in which a person has trouble with social interaction and communication with other people, among other symptoms.

background check A process in which resources like police databases and registry of motor vehicle records are checked to ensure that a person has not committed any violations that indicate he or she might endanger the children in his or her care.

brick-and-mortar A company that has physical premises, as opposed to an online-only company.

cardiopulmonary resuscitation (CPR) Emergency medical procedures that are done on someone whose breathing or heartbeat has stopped, for example, after an electric shock, heart attack, or drowning. CPR combines rescue breathing and chest compressions.

child development The process of enhancing children's physical, social, and intellectual skills.

curriculum The collection of classes taught in a school.

early learning Activities designed to help children develop physical, social, and intellectual skills before they start elementary school.

government subsidy A sum of money paid to a person or organization to provide services.

66

Head Start A government program designed to provide underprivileged preschool-aged children with the skills to succeed in school.

hospice A health care facility in which patients with terminal illnesses are provided with comfort care.

incurable Unable to be cured, likely to lead to death.

infirm Having a condition of weakness or illness that usually lasts for a long time and is caused especially by old age; people who are weak or ill.

latchkey children Children who are left on their own after school, usually because their parents are at work. Called "latchkey" because they are given a key to let themselves into their house after school.

multicultural From a variety of ethnic and cultural backgrounds.

overhead The expenses necessary to run an organization, such as rent, electricity, heat, and the like.

phishing A technique used by Internet scammers to get people to provide personal information that can be used for identity theft.

portfolio A collection of material that illustrates a person's accomplishments in his or her field.

professionalism Behaving according to the standards of one's field and in a manner that inspires respect.

program management The process of tracking and controlling projects.

psychological Related to mental functions.

standards Guidelines for behavior and performance established by an authoritative industry organization.

synagogue A Jewish house of worship. Also called a temple.

tax break A discount on income tax given to individuals or organizations that meet specific criteria.

for more information

Canadian Child Care Federation (CCCF)
700 Industrial Avenue, Suite 600
Ottawa, ON K1G 0Y9
Canada
(613) 729-5289 or (800) 858-1412
Website: http://www.cccf-fcsge.ca
The CCCF provides information, professional development
    resources, and publications for child care professionals in
    Canada.

Canadian Nanny Association (CNA)
2343 Brimley Road, Suite 886
Toronto, ON M1S 3L6
Canada
(416) 479-3663
Website: http://www.nannyone.org
The CNA offers support and resources for nannies in Canada.

Center for the Child Care Workforce (CCW)
555 New Jersey Avenue NW
Washington, DC 20001
(202) 662-8005
Website: http://www.ccw.org
The CCW provides data and resources, including a newsletter
    for child care workers.

Child Care Aware of America
U.S. Department of Health and Human Services
1515 North Courthouse Road, 11th Floor
Arlington, VA 22201

(800) 424-2246
Website: http://www.childcareaware.org/child-care-providers
This group gives out information for those planning to
become child care providers, including a variety of
resources on its website.

Child Life Council, Inc. (CLC)
11821 Parklawn Drive, Suite 310
Rockville, MD 20852-2539
(301) 881-7090 or (800) 252-4515
Website: http://www.childlife.org
The CLC supports child life professionals as they empower
children and families to master challenging events related
to health care. It provides a variety of resources, including
some for students.

Council for Professional Recognition
2460 16th Street NW
Washington, DC 20009-3547
(202) 265-9090 or (800) 424-4310
Website: http://www.cdacouncil.org
This council provides certification for child care professionals.

InterExchange
161 Sixth Avenue
New York, NY 10013
(212) 924-0446
Website: http://www.interexchange.org/working-abroad
A nonprofit organization, InterExchange is an au pair agency
that places Americans abroad.

National Association for the Education of Young Children
(NAEYC)
1313 L Street NW, Suite 500

Washington, DC 20005
(202) 232-8777
Website: http://www.naeyc.org
The NAEYC provides resources to support child care professionals teaching children from babies to age eight.

National Resource Center for Health and Safety in Child
    Care and Early Education (NRC)
13120 East 19th Avenue, Mail Stop F541
P.O. Box 6511
Aurora, CO 80045
(800) 598-5437
Website: http://nrckids.org
The NRC seeks to improve the quality of child care and early
    education programs by supporting child care providers
    and early educators, families, health professionals, early
    childhood comprehensive systems, state child care regula-
    tory agencies, state and local health departments, and
    policy makers in their efforts to identify and promote
    healthy and safe child care and early education programs.
    It provides a variety of online and print resources.

Office of Child Care (OCC)
Administration for Children and Families
U.S. Department of Health and Human Services
370 L'Enfant Promenade SW
Washington, DC 20447
(202) 690-6782
Website: http://www.acf.hhs.gov/programs/occ
The OCC supports low-income working families through
    child care financial assistance and promotes children's
    learning by improving the quality of early care and educa-
    tion and after-school programs. It provides resources for
    child care providers.

U.S. Bureau of Labor Statistics (BLS)
Division of Information and Marketing Services
2 Massachusetts Avenue NE, Room 2850
Washington, DC 20212
(202) 691-5200
Website: http://www.bls.gov
The BLS is the U.S. Department of Labor agency that is
   responsible for measuring labor market activity and
   collecting important economic information about jobs
   and the U.S. workforce. It provides career guides to and
   statistics on careers in various industries. (For data on
   child care, see http://www.bls.gov/ooh/Personal-Care
   -and-Service/Childcare-workers.htm.)

WEBSITES

Because of the changing nature of Internet links, Rosen
Publishing has developed an online list of websites related to
the subject of this book. This site is updated regularly. Please
use this link to access the list:

http://www.rosenlinks.com/ECAR/Chil

for further reading

Boone, Beverly. *Basic Training for Residential Child Care Workers: A Practical Guide for Improving Services to Children.* Springfield, IL: Charles C. Thomas, 2012.

Bruce, Tina, Carolyn Megitt, and Julian Grenier. *Child Care and Education.* London, England: Hodder Education, 2010.

Byers, Ann. *Great Resume, Application, and Interview Skills* (Work Readiness). New York, NY: Rosen Publishing, 2008.

Christen, Carol, and Richard N. Bolles. *What Color Is Your Parachute for Teens: Discovering Yourself, Defining Your Future.* 2nd ed. New York, NY: Ten Speed Press/Random House, 2010.

Cryer, Shelly. *The Nonprofit Career Guide: How to Land a Job That Makes a Difference.* Nashville, TN: Fieldstone Alliance, 2008.

Eberts, Marjorie, and Margaret Gisler. *Careers for Kids at Heart and Others Who Adore Children.* New York, NY: McGraw-Hill, 2006.

Fry, Ron. *101 Great Answers to the Toughest Interview Questions.* Boston, MA: Course Technology, 2009.

Henneberg, Susan. *Money-Making Opportunities for Teens Who Like Working with Kids* (Make Money Now!). New York, NY: Rosen Publishing, 2014.

Kennedy, Joyce Lain. *Cover Letters for Dummies.* Hoboken, NJ: Wiley Publishing, 2009.

Kennedy, Joyce Lain. *Job Interviews for Dummies.* Hoboken, NJ: Wiley Publishing, 2011.

Kennedy, Joyce Lain. *Resumes for Dummies.* Hoboken, NJ: Wiley Publishing, 2011.

Kensington, Emma. *The Best Nanny Handbook: The Ultimate Guide for Nannies*. Seattle, WA: Createspace, 2008.

Lore, Nicholas. *Now What? The Young Person's Guide to Choosing the Perfect Career*. New York, NY: Fireside/Simon & Schuster, 2008.

Minett, Pamela. *Child Care & Development*. London, England: Hodder Education, 2010.

Peterson's. *Teens' Guide to College and Career Planning*. Lawrenceville, NJ: Peterson's, 2011.

Suen, Anastasia. *Getting a Job in Child Care* (Job Basics: Getting the Job You Need). New York, NY: Rosen Publishing, 2014.

Vescia, Monique. *Social Network–Powered Employment Opportunities* (A Teen's Guide to the Power of Social Networking). New York, NY: Rosen Publishing, 2014.

bibliography

Adams, Susan. "Confessions of the Best Nanny in the World." *Forbes*, April 4, 2013. Retrieved January 3, 2014 (http://www.forbes.com/sites/susanadams/2013/04/04/confessions-of-the-best-nanny-in-the-world).

Berfield, Susan. "Many Jobs in Nanny Economy, Few Qualified Applicants." *Bloomberg BusinessWeek*, September 7, 2012. Retrieved January 3, 2014 (http://www.businessweek.com/articles/2012-09-07/many-jobs-in-nanny-economy-few-qualified-applicants).

Carpenter, Rachel. "Sample Interview Questions for a Child Care or Day Care Worker." Retrieved December 27, 2013 (http://voices.yahoo.com/sample-job-interview-questions-child-care-or-11936998.html).

Child Life Council. "Certification for the Child Life Profession." Retrieved December 23, 2013 (http://www.childlife.org/Certification).

ChildStats.gov. "America's Children: Key National Indicators of Well-Being, 2013." Retrieved December 18, 2013 (http://www.childstats.gov/americaschildren/famsoc3.asp).

Chuck, Elizabeth. "Modern-day Mary Poppins: College Graduates Embrace Nannying as Career." NBC News, September 11, 2013. Retrieved January 2, 2014 (http://www.nbcnews.com/#/news/other/modern-day-mary-poppins-college-graduates-embrace-nannying-career-f8C11131010).

Council for Professional Education. "How to Earn the Child Development Associate Certification." Retrieved December 26, 2013 (http://www.nannynetwork.com/Library/NannyLib/FindNannyJob.cfm).

Eberts, Marjorie, and Margaret Gisler. *Careers in Child Care*. 3rd ed. New York, NY: McGraw-Hill, 2008.

Finn, Lisa. "Child Care Worker Duties." *Houston Chronicle.*
    Retrieved December 26, 2013 (http://everydaylife.globalpost
    .com/child-care-worker-duties-2119.html).
International Nanny Association. "Recommended Practices
    for Nannies." Retrieved January 2, 2014 (http://www
    .nanny.org/recommended-practices#soyou).
Kennsington, Emma. *The Best Nanny Handbook: The Ultimate
    Guide For Nannies.* Seattle, WA: CreateSpace, 2008.
Krow, Shailynn. "Child Care Qualifications." *Houston Chronicle.*
    Retrieved December 26, 2013 (http://work.chron.com/
    child-care-worker-qualifications-12570.html).
LaRowe, Michelle, and Sarah McCormack-Hoffman. *Beyond
    Parenting Basics: The International Nanny Association's Official
    Guide to In-Home Child Care.* Charlotte, NC: International
    Nanny Association, 2009.
Laubenthal, Kristen. *A Nanny's Day—The Professional Way!
    A Curriculum Book for the Professional Early Childhood
    Nanny.* Bloomington, IN: AuthorHouse, 2012.
Malcolm, Melanie Paige. *Changing Diapers for Profit! A Fun
    Program for Home Daycare Providers.* Seattle, WA:
    CreateSpace, 2010.
Meadows, Scott. *Daycare Building Blocks for a Highly Profitable
    Childcare Business.* Seattle, WA: CreateSpace, 2014.
Michel, Sonya. "Child Care: The American History: The
    History of Child Care in the U.S." The Social History
    Project. Retrieved December 14, 2013 (http://www
    .socialwelfarehistory.com/programs/child-care-the
    -american-history).
Murray, Kris. *The Ultimate Child Care Marketing Guide:
    Tactics, Tools, and Strategies for Success.* St. Paul, MN:
    Redleaf Press, 2012.
NannyNetwork.com. "How to Find a Nanny Job." Retrieved
    January 2, 2014 (http://www.nannynetwork.com/Library/
    NannyLib/FindNannyJob.cfm).

Princeton Review. "Career: Child Care Worker." Retrieved December 23, 2013 (http://www.princetonreview.com/careers.aspx?cid=35).

Savage, Bernard. *How to Start a Home-Based Day-Care Business!* Seattle, WA: CreateSpace, 2013.

Sciarra, Dorothy Jean. *Developing and Administering a Child Care and Education Program.* Belmont, CA: Wadsworth/Cengage Learning, 2012.

Segal, Marilyn, M. Kori Bardige, Lorraine Breffni, and Mary Jean Woika. *All About Child Care and Early Education: A Comprehensive Resource for Child Care Professionals.* Upper Saddle River, NJ: Pearson, 2011.

Steelsmith, Shari. *How to Start a Home-Based Day-Care Business.* 6th ed. Guilford, CT: Globe Pequot Press, 2011.

Steward, Peggy. *Childcare Revealed.* Pensacola, FL: Jamison Street Preschool, 2010.

Thompson, Molly. "Strengths as a Child Care Worker." *Houston Chronicle.* Retrieved December 23, 2013 (http://work.chron.com/strengths-child-care-worker-10114.html).

U.S. Bureau of Labor Statistics. "Childcare Workers." *Occupational Outlook Handbook.* Retrieved December 19, 2013 (http://www.bls.gov/ooh/Personal-Care-and-Service/Childcare-workers.htm).

U.S. Department of Health and Human Services. "Number and Characteristics of Early Care and Education (ECE) Teachers and Caregivers: Initial Findings from the National Survey of Early Care and Education (NSECE)." Retrieved December 21, 2013 (http://www.acf.hhs.gov/sites/default/files/opre/nsece_wf_brief_102913_0.pdf).

index

A

after-school programs, 13, 14, 22
American Red Cross, 48
au pairs, 11, 33

B

babysitting, 33, 42
background checks, 28, 58, 60
business managers of child care
    centers, 27

C

Canadian Child Care
    Federation, 29
CareerBuilder.com, 55
Certified Child Care Professional
    certification, 49
Certified Child Life Professional
    exam, 51–52
child care, history of, 7–10
child care associates, aides, and
    assistants, 13, 20, 21–22
child care jobs/careers
    education needed, 6, 13, 25,
        40–52
    future growth/outlook of, 11
    how to find, 53–60
    job security, 5

skills needed for, 27–28
turnover in, 53, 55
in your own home, 13, 16,
    28–29
Child Development Associate
    certification, 48
Child Life Council, 51
child life specialists, 13, 30–32, 46,
    51–52
corporate/in-house child care
    centers, 13, 15
Council for Professional
    Recognition, 48
CPR/first aid, 46, 48, 51, 63

D

day care facilities, 11, 13, 14–19
directors of child care centers, 11,
    13, 21, 25–27

E

education
    certification, 48–52
    college training, 44–48
    high school preparation, 40–43
eNannySource.com, 58
extended-day child care centers, 16

F

4nannies.com, 58

77

ABOUT THE AUTHOR

Jeri Freedman has a B.A. degree from Harvard University. For several years, she worked in the education department of the Anti-Defamation League, a position in which she participated in the training of history teachers. She is the author of numerous young adult nonfiction books, including *Women in the Workplace: Wages, Respect, and Equal Rights* and *Being a Leader: Organizing and Inspiring a Group.* She has also written books about careers in the fields of security, human resources, sports management and administration, computer technology, and pharmaceutical sales.

PHOTO CREDITS

Cover, p. 1 (figures) LjupcoSmokovski/Shutterstock.com; cover, p. 1 (background) zu difeng/Shutterstock.com; pp. 4–5, 12, 16–17, 22, 26–27, 31, 42, 44–45, 46-47 © AP Images; p. 8 © Mary Evans Picture Library/The Images Works; p. 10 Library of Congress Prints and Photographs Division; p. 15 RJ Sangosti/The Denver Post/Getty Images; p. 19 The Washington Post/Getty Images; p. 24 The Chicago Tribune/McClatchy-Tribune/Getty Images; p. 29 Tacoma News Tribune/McClatchy-Tribune/Getty Images; pp. 34–35 The Boston Globe/Getty Images; p. 37 Bloomberg/Getty Images; p. 38 Tiburon Studios/E+/Getty Images; p 41 © Joel Koyama/Minneapolis Star Tribune/ZUMAPress; pp. 50–51 Mike Cardew/MCT/Landov; p. 54 Monkey Business Images/Thinkstock; pp. 56–57 © Ringo Chiu/ZUMAPress; p 59 Digital Vision/Photodisc/Thinkstock.

Designer: Matt Cauli; Editor: Kathy Kuhtz Campbell; Photo Researcher: Amy Feinberg